ODE TO A
BLACK QUEEN

God's Greatest Creation

Rashaad Singleton

Dedication

This book is dedicated to my mother and every black goddess in the world. Never give up, never surrender. I love you all.

Prelude

Why am I writing this book? Because it needed to be written. Because it is long overdue. How long do I have to hear about the achievements of white women, while at the same time, we hear only a small amount of the MANY achievements of black women? Where are the legendary figures that look like my sisters, and my mother and my grandmother? Surely, we had Queens too. Oh, but that's just it isn't it? White supremacy would have us believe that our first ancestral mothers began their existence as slaves and handmaids for white folk. Well, that's a bold face lie and in this book, we're going to talk about it.... The most devastating assault by white supremacy upon black women was manipulating them to think that their beautiful shades of brown was anything less than perfect. The black woman has always been and will always be, the epitome of eternal beauty. Each shade is a direct reflection of her divine connection with God. Writing this book was very emotional for me, because the more I understand the black woman, the more I love the black woman. The more I researched the black woman, the more I was in awe of the black woman. Once one fully understands the history of black women, it becomes quite clear, that she is 2nd to none. Then it occurred to me, that this is why white supremacy spends billions of dollars miseducating the black woman. They willfully refuse to teach us about Black Queens in history, and if they do manage to squeeze some history in, it's not with the same enthusiasm that is used when teaching about European queens. Anyone who objects to that is clearly in denial. Why is that the case though? Are we not "allowed' to see our royal ancestors in a positive light? Or would they have us continue to believe that old racist narrative that all of our ancestors came from swinging vines in the jungle? Are we supposed to continue to believe that we came from the jungles of Africa, went to picking cotton and being their house servants? Please. American education is a joke, a racist joke at that. They want our queens, both past and present, to be left totally neglected, unprotected and assuredly, they want her to be the most disrespected. That ends now. They don't teach us this is school, but in this book we are going to talk about it....

Table of Contents

Dr. Frances Cress Welsing

Chapter 1:   Perseverance

When you think of powerful black queens today, many names come to mind. There is Michelle Obama, Oprah, Beyonce, and many more. It has to be understood that this is not anything new. As soon as black people were freed from the confinement of chattel slavery, there were many that became millionaires in just a few decades. Imagine how great we would have been if white supremacy did not have us bound down to picking cotton and tending to the needs of their families for centuries. If black women could turn themselves into millionaires right out of slavery, imagine if that slavery never existed. What if we had spent centuries tending to the well-being of our own families and our own communities without having to do the same for our oppressors. How much further would we be? What if our precious women were not mistreated and abused by slave masters? How much mentally healthier would our communities and relationships be? For instance, a slave master or overseer would force himself on the wife or a daughter of a man and if the man fought back, he was killed. If he didn't fight back, the relationship was killed. This was a normal day in white America. This behavior did not stop in slavery. The next form of slavery was sharecropping. Most black men worked in the fields while their wife would be hired as a house maid. Many white farmers would force themselves on their black maids and threaten that if she told anyone, he would fire her and the husband, or worse, lynch them both. The pressure would now be put on the women to make a decision. It was the goal of many white farmers to make black women choose between not having a job or get abused while having a job. It's circumstances like this that proves since the beginning of this nation, black women have been the least appreciated and most disrespected, when she should be the most appreciated and the most respected.

The black Queen is a national treasure. Look at what she has gone through. She has been in chains while simultaneously nursing the babies of slave masters and her own children. That's quite the superhero. Just imagine, it was very common for a black woman to have a white baby feeding on one of her breasts and her own baby feeding on the other. Most white mothers would tell their slaves to make sure the babies didn't use the same nipple, basically comparing the black woman's breasts to a "white only/ colored" water fountain. However, there is no records of white women breastfeeding black babies. If it was not for the breastmilk of Black mothers, many white babies would have starved to death. I don't see no white people thanking her for that though. Where's that holiday? Nobody wants to talk about that, but the historical photos are proof.

Yes, we all should thank the black women when we see her, for no reason at all. We should just just thank her for existing. We should bow down and humble ourselves in her presence. For if it was not for her, no man, black or white or red or brown, would be here. Through all her pain, the black women continue to set the example of what grace and elegance is. Where most would have given up, the black Queen continues to move forward, and she has been doing so for a mighty long time.

Dr. Joy DeGruy

Queen Amanirenas

Chapter 2:   Queen Amanirenas

All of our lives, we are taught about all of the royal figures of Europe. However, how did the scholars forget to teach us about the great Queens of Kush. The title of the Kush Queens was Kandake or Candance. They ruled Kush with their husbands and sons. A Candance was so powerful in Kush, that if her son was not doing a great job at being King, she had the power to remove him from office. When they ruled with their husband, they had the same amount of power in rulership as he did. What was most remarkable about the Kandake Queens was that when they went to war with their enemies, the queens did not stay at home and wait in a castle. No, they led the armies from the front. They were on the front line inspiring every man around them.

The greatest of these black queens was named Queen Amanirenas. She was the 2nd queen of Kush also known as Nubia. She ruled the kingdom between 40 B.C and 10 B.C. It was the area between southern Egypt and Sudan. It was during her rule, that Kush would wage war with the greatest military in the world at the time, the Roman Empire. However, she didn't just wage war with them...she won.

When Cleopatra died, Rome took complete control of Egypt also known as "Kemet". They decided to tax the Nubians. This was done basically to establish dominance over them and Queen Amanirenas. Well, the Queen did not have it, but she didn't want to disturb the peace because she understood what the consequences would be if she went to war with Rome. However, as usual, white supremacy is never satisfied, so Rome begins to take up more and more territory. Well eventually, they arrived at the border of the Kush Empire. They thought they were going just to continue to rob and acquire land, but unfortunately for them, they reached an area that was ruled by a group of Black Queens that did not play any games, whatsoever.

After hearing about this breach, Queen Amanirenas gathered her army and invaded the Roman territory. On her arrival, she found a statue of the Roman emperor, Augustus. She chopped off the damn head and took it back to her house. She then took the head to the temple and buried it at the front entrance. She did that so that everyone who entered the temple had to step on the face of Augustus. She did this to show Rome that she was not to be played with. Mind you, Rome had the largest military in the world at that time.

On top of that pettiness, she sent messengers to Rome with gifts. When they arrived, they presented the Emperor with a bundle of golden arrows attached with a message. The message said, "if you want peace, accept these golden arrows as a peace offering, but if you war, keep them because you will need them." As time went on, Rome continued their conquest for land and territory and eventually Queen Amanarenis had had enough. She declared war on Rome and immediately took control of 3 Roman cities.

Her army was only 30,000, while the Roman military was 120,000 minimum. This queen mother did not care about the numbers though. She cared about protecting her people from colonizing invaders. She was such a warrior that she was blinded in one eye during battle. After her injury, she rested a little while, healed up, and went right back into action on to the battle field with just one eye. Even the history of Rome records the history of a one eyed Nubian Queen leading troops into battle. What kind of superhero is that? Black children need to hear this history before they ever hear one detail of European history. For 3 years Queen Amanirenas waged war with the Roman Empire, and after 3 years, she won! The Roman Empire knew that defeat was near and begged for a peace treaty. They discontinued their tax on the Kush empire. Queen Amanirenas and her Kingdom was completely free from colonialism and white supremacy. A black woman went to war and and beat one of the greatest militaries of all time and she did so, with one eye. If she did it once, she can it do again.

Queen Amanirenas

Queen of Sheba

Chapter 3:   Queen Makeda and Queen Zewditu

What is this attack on our young black girls that a government would deny the images and history of women who have the ability to empower them? Is it because they don't want our black girls to see themselves as Royal figures? Is it not enough that white supremacy portrays God as white? Is it not enough that white supremacy displayed all the angels as white? Is it not enough that they made all the prophets of the Bible white? White America ignores our history and the part they do tell, they white-wash it. That makes that two separate, but equally effective psychological genocides.

When you think of the Queens of Europe, what do you think of? Gold? Diamonds? Servants? Now, please try and remember one Black Queen that you learned about in grade school. Probably none. This is a historical genocide. How could we not be taught about the great queens of Africa such as the Queens of Ethiopia, Queen Makeda and Empress Zewditu? The Queen of Sheba, which meant Queen of the South, was the sole leader of Ethiopia. The Queen's royal name was Makeda. Her beauty was known throughout the land and she was considered the gorgeous creation of her time. She was a dark, rich in melanin, Queen and she flaunted it proudly. She was wealthy beyond measure and her entire Kingdom adored her and was loyal to her with their lives. During her reign, she decided to visit Israel. She had heard that there was a king there who claimed to be the wisest man in the world. His name was King Solomon, the same King Solomon of the Bible. People think they got money today, compared to Queen Makeda, they don't have anything. As a gift for King Solomon, she gave him spices and jewels and 7,200 lbs of gold. Yes, thousands and thousands of pounds of gold as a gift.

Well, to test the the wisdom of King Solomon, Queen Makeda decided to ask him some very tough questions. However, King Solomon had an answer for all of them. Queen Makeda was very impressed that King Solomon had lived up to the hype. They would continue to go back and forth and eventually, the battle of wits became a flirtatious exchange. It probably was then and there that she fell in love with the King. King Solomon had been smitten as well. They were rumored to have a child who would become later become King of Ethiopia and continue the royal bloodline of Israel. Ethiopia from that time on would accept Judaism/ Christianity as their national religious faith. It should be noted that this was done before they had encountered any Europeans powers practicing it.

The Queen of Sheba was obviously black, but Europeans always try to depict her as white. This is an attack on black culture. First off, common damn sense tells you that Ethiopia is in Africa. Ethiopia is the oldest known country in the world with the most ancient people. Although they were invaded by Italy, they are still the only African country never to be fully colonized by a European power. The people are black today and they were black in the days of King Solomon. Some Biblical scholars predict the Songs of Solomon are in fact about the relationship of King Solomon and Queen Makeda. If so, that would make sense because King Solmon is smitten over this woman and the woman is quoted in saying, "I am black, but comely (beautifu), O ye daughters of Jerusalem, as the tents of Kedar, as the curtains of Solomon. Look not upon me, because I am black, because the sun hath looked upon me: my mother's children were angry with me; they made me the keeper of the vineyards;" Solomon 1:5-6. The Bible also gives a clear description that the Jews are black as well. "Judah mourneth, and the gates thereof languish; they are black unto the ground; and the cry of Jerusalem is gone up." -Jeremiah 14:2 However, for whatever reason, white supremacy keeps giving us white images after white images.

Now Europeans have historically always made attempts to white-wash black history, especially the black Pharos of Egypt. They did the same thing with Queen Makeda. They would have kept doing it, but they made one mistake; they invented the camera.

They can paint over paintings, but it's hard to white-wash a photograph. Empress Zewditu of Ethiopia understood this and always took stunning pictures. Her Royal Majesty Empress Zewditu was born on April 29, 1876. While she had very important advisers around her, she reigned as sole ruler of Ethiopia from Sept 27, 1916 to April 2, 1930. She was the successor of King Lij Iyasu and the predecessor of his royal majesty, King Halie Selassie. She bore the name "Nigiste Negest", which literally meant Queen of Kings. This name was given to her to make clear; no one was to ever have a higher title than her for as long as she lived. She was very influential in helping Ethiopia become modernized from their old traditional system that seems to be behind western powers. Although she wanted to modernize Ethiopia, she still valued the cultural traditions that made them the unique people that they were. She was extremely religious and she devoted most her time to fasting and prayer. She was very elegant beyond words. However, the images of her royalty are left out of western history books. What would it have done for the morale of our grandmothers who was born in 1920s if they knew that there was a black Queen in Ethiopia at the same time that was showered in gold and diamonds? No black southern woman had seen such a sight as Queen Zewditu. The closest image they had to royalty was merely entertainers whose wealth did not compare to the treasury of Ethiopia. White supremacy hides those images, but they don't mind showing us the images of black American women in slavery though. They showed us that, but how did they not show us this? It was all intentionally done. Just the mere images of Queen Zewditu could have revolutionized minds. They enthusiastically taught us about the royalty of Europe, but when did they teach us about Queen Zewditu? To hide the images of the black Queens of Ethiopia is a crime and an attack on the very conscious of black people worldwide. After all, had it not been for the royal class of people in Africa, there would have never been a royal class for Europe to copy from.

Queen Zewditu

ANN ZINGHA.

Queen of Matamba.

The original of this picture, painted on parchment, is to be found in Brazil in a convent of Capuchins.

Queen Nzinga

Chapter 4: Europeans, you don't know what's good

There is no secret that every black Queen has a warrior spirit inside of her. It's an uncontrollable urge to protect no matter what the costs may be. This was evident during the Transatlantic Slave Trade. Portugal, along with Spain and England decided that they wanted to enslave all black people in the world. On the 18th of June 1452, Pope Nicholas V and the Catholic Church signed the Dum Diverse, a papal bull that subjugated all non-Christians, which was all African people, to slavery from birth to death. Europeans thought they would have the final word on that matter, but there was one Black Queen in Angola who was not trying to hear any of that. Her name was Queen Nzinga.

Queen Nzinga was born in 1583. Her father was King Ngola Kiluanji of the Ndongo tribe. Her mother was Kangela Kiluangi and was a former slave who captured the heart of the King. Once again, the story of Queen Nzinga is ignored in the American education system, but they see fit to teach young black girls all about the white queens and princesses of Europe. Ignoring the history of a people when you have the ability to teach it is an offense on their self-esteem. White America purposefully leaves out the stories of black queens to kill the self-worth in our young girls. The amazing story of Queen Nzinga cannot be hidden forever though.

From birth, she was a fighter. It is said that when she was born, the umbilical cord was wrapped around her neck. She literally had to fight just to get out of the wound. Queen Nzinga was living in the age when the Transatlantic Slave Trade was in full effect. Europeans, starting with the Portuguese was ravishing Africa of its people and its resources. During the time of her father's rule, the Portuguese military population and power were growing in Angola rapidly and it was becoming an uncomfortable force for everyone. This was systematic and is a perfect example of how white supremacy works. First, they sent the missionaries. Secondly, they sent the merchants. Then they sent the military to appear to be protecting the merchants, but in reality, they were sending the military to take up more African territory. That's exactly what had happened in Angola. Now, Queen Nzinga had 3 siblings. Her brother was Mbandi. Her 2 sisters were Kifungi and Mukambu. Nzinga was the oldest. Naturally, it would be fitting in those days for her brother to take the throne after her father, but research shows he had little desire for military tactics or politics. It was Nzinga who had been molded by her father since birth to govern and rule a nation. She was a master at hunting and warfare. She had been trained to understand the world of politics and how it operates. The difference between Nzinga's training and her brother's training was the fact that she actually loved it, unlike her brother. It was clear who needed to be the leader of the nation. She even spoke and wrote in Portuguese fluently. Although she was the daughter of the King, her mother was from another tribe. This caused an uprise amongst the people about her legitimacy to the throne. However, she was her father's pride and joy. From a young age, he allowed her to witness how to govern in his day to day affairs. He even carried her to war. How's that for a "daddy daughter work day"? So, the reader can imagine how much the king must have adored her to take so much time to teach her about rulership. This might be due to a wise woman who told the King and his wife at Nzinga's birth, "she will be Queen someday". He obviously took that message to heart.

King Ngola Kiluanji was a fierce King as well. Surely, it must have had a huge impact on Nzinga because she did not play any games. When the Portuguese arrived to Angola, they had one priority, to capture and enslave the Mbandu people. Some Mbandu tribes made deals with the Portuguese. However, Kiluangi was not persuaded to make any deals with Europeans because he knew that they were impossible to trust. However, due to the fact the surrounding territories were making deals, the Portuguese begin to get closer and closer to Ndongo territory. The king had had enough. He declared war on Portugal. In 1617, King Kiluanji died. Before he died, Nzinga promised that she would keep the white foreigners out their land. His son, Mbandi, would take the throne and would be the sole ruler of the land. Unfortunately, everyone doubted his abilities to rule, even Queen Nzinga herself. Even the common people knew this, but they dared not to speak on it. Anyone who opposed his rulership was put to death. Queen Nzinga's son and mother was killed because of this. Nzinga would have also been murdered, but she was so beloved by the people that the King knew if she was harmed, it would have been all out chaos amongst the people.

So instead, she became the official representative of King Mbandi. However, many people including the Portuguese saw her to be the true Queen of Angola. The Portuguese founded a city in Angola called Luanda which is the current capital of Angola today. She was invited to Luanda to meet the Portuguese governor and discuss terms of peace. She agreed and took a caravan of people with her. When she arrived, she was disrespected from the jump. The Governor sat high in a royal chair and on the floor laid a pillow. Queen Nzinga questioned what it was?

The Governor said, "that's your seat." She responded that that is something for servants to sit on and that she was no servant. She demanded a chair, and the Governor refused to give her one. This is the audacity of white supremacy. He wanted to look down at her and wanted her to physically look up at him. Queen Nzinga was not in the mood for any shenanigans though. The rude governor obviously had no idea of who he was fooling with. She called one of her servants over and he got on his hands and knees made himself into a chair. Queen Nzinga then proceeded to take her seat. She did this not to humiliate the servant, but to show that she was just as powerful as the governor and more loved by the people. The Governor got a reality check that he was not just talking to some everyday person, he was talking to a Black Queen. The meeting commenced and they were able to work out a peace treaty.

As time went on, the pressure of rulership grew too heavy for King Mbandi and he committed suicide. With no leader appointed, the Portuguese saw that as a perfect opportunity to attack and so they did. Queen Nzinga and her people had to flee to the mountains. She was very angry at the betrayal and lies of the Portuguese after peace terms had already been agreed upon. As time passed on, Queen Nzinga was able to reorganize and she built up an army to fight. She made up her mind that she was going to keep the Portuguese out of her land or die trying. Eventually, Queen Nzinga made an alliance with the Dutch to help fight the Portuguese and it worked. Her power and leadership could not be denied any longer. Nzinga was declared Ngola Kiluanji of Mbandu people. Her closest confidants were her sisters. She was the first woman to be the sole leader of the Mbandu people and lived up to all of her expectations. After she became Queen, women became more important in Angolan society immediately and she even appointed women in her cabinets and urged many to join the military.

(Map of Angola)

Queen Nzinga was truly a warrior Queen. She didn't just declare war on the Portuguese, she led the fight in it. The Portuguese tried to kill Queen Nzinga on many occasions and they failed time after time again. For 40 long years, Queen Nzinga fought the Portuguese. As long as she lived, the Portuguese could never gain full control of Angola. No European man stood a chance if they were in her way. All were slain, one after another. The death toll is unknown, but for the war to last 40 years and you win, one can imagine.

If this was common knowledge, what would this do to the minds of millions of black girls in America and across the world? What if they knew there was a black Queen in Angola who seem to be invincible and destroyed every enemy that came in her path? She was a "super hero' before the phrase was ever created. Hollywood has shown our black queens on the slave plantations, but they sure did leave out the history of Queen Nzinga. Is she not important? How could she not be when she fought off white supremacy for almost half a century? These are the heroes that are essential to the minds of black women who have to learn how to appreciate themselves because they live in society that purposely devalues them through media and the distortion of history. Queen Nzinga is most remembered for one of her most interesting quotes, "Europeans, you don't know what's good."

Queen Nzinga

Queen Naa Asantewaa

Chapter 5: Golden Stool

During the times of the Transatlantic Slave Trade, life was very difficult. The Portuguese were colonizing Angola and the English were colonizing west Africa. In West Africa, there was a powerful empire known as the Ashanti Kingdom. They were a group of African people who had migrated to Ghana. Many people believe that the origin of the Ashanti Kingdom is in fact Israel. What supports this theory is the very name "Ashanti" itself. If you break down the word, the "ti" on the end of Ashanti, it means the "Children of". So, it's literally means the children of Ashun. Within the Bible, the Ashun are a group of Israelites out of the Tribe of Judah and they are mentioned specifically by name.

Joshua 15:1 and 42

1.This then was the lot of the tribe of the children of Judah by their families; even to the border of Edom the wilderness of Zin southward was the uttermost part of the south coast.

42. Libnah, and Ether, and Ashan,"

They were colonized by the British in the 1800's. When the English first met the Ashanti Tribe, they noticed immediately that they had strange customs compared to the other local African tribes. For an example, they circumcised their children on a certain day which was a distinct Israelite custom. The majority of Hamites and Gentiles did not practice circumcision. So right away, the English knew the Ashanti were a different people. What solidified it was the high priest of the of the Ashanti Tribe. He wore a plate around his neck with 12 stones. This was identical to a scripture in the Bible.

"There shall be twelve stones with their names according to the names of the sons of Israel. They shall be like signets, each engraved with its name, for the twelve tribes."- Exodus 28:21

The British sought out to crush the Ashanti empire because they rejected European oppression and were also great warriors. One of their greatest leaders that has ever lived was Queen Mother, Yaa Asantewaa who led a war against the British at the age of 60.

Born in 1840, Yaa Asantewaaa was a member of the Royal Family of the Ashanti Kingdom. During the time she lived, the British were attacking all of the surrounding areas. She had witnessed the destruction of her Kingdom due to these foreign invaders and she had finally had enough. The King of the Ashanti had been defeated and exiled to the Seychelles, a group of islands that were used as holding cells. The British Governor, Sir Fredrick Hodgson, was not satisfied though. He wanted more. He wanted to completely crush the spirit of Ashanti Kingdom and in order to do that, he had to have the Ashanti's most prize possession, The Golden Stool. The Golden Stool was a solid gold stool that The Ashanti Kingdom believed harvested all of the souls of the Ashanti people. It was a stool, but no one, not even the King himself, was allowed to sit on it. To put it into perspective, even the Golden Stool had a stool to sit on. They treasured the Golden Stool more than life itself. However, white supremacy is bold and has no limits. Sir Fredrick Hodgson did the unthinkable. He called a meeting with the leaders of the Ashanti Tribe and demanded that they allow him to sit on the Golden Stool. Not only that, he also wanted to own it. The Ashanti people were enraged. The men in charge decided to discuss the pros and cons of giving up their most prize possession. The very attempt to negotiate put Yaa Asantewaa in a great rage. The men become silent. Yaa Asantewaa was disgusted. She no longer recognized the tribe that she had been brought up in. She knew the Ashanti Kingdom was a kingdom of warriors and yet was ready to compromise without a fight. The white Europeans wanted the Golden Stool and to the Ashanti empire that was the "Soul of their nation". To ask for that was a declaration of war. Yaa Asantewaa obliged and called a meeting.

In her speech, she says,

Now I have seen that some of you fear to go forward to fight for our king. If it were in the brave days of, the days of Osei Tutu, Okomfo Anokye, and Opoku Ware, leaders would not sit down to see their king taken away without firing a shot.
No white man could have dared to speak to chief of the Ashanti in the way the Governor spoke to you leaders this morning. Is it true that the bravery of the Ashanti is no more? I cannot believe it. It cannot be! I must say this: if you the men of Ashanti will not go forward, then we will. We, the women will. I shall call upon my fellow women.
We will fight the white men. We will fight till the last of us falls in the battlefields."

When Yaa Asantewaa declared war, all hell broke loose. There were 2 sides, you were either on the Ashanti side or you were marked for dead. Her top priority was to capture and arrest the governor who had asked to sit on the Golden Stool. She put a hit out on his head. Many British government workers and missionaries went to seek refuge in a church. The walls of the church were so thick, it was able to withstand the Ashanti bullets. However, Yaa

Asantewaa was a superb general. She knew that eventually; the British would run out of bullets and on top of that she cut off on the entire food supply to the Church. The colonists were dying in heavy numbers. The English general that was at the fort was able to escape with his wife and a few men after a period of time and eventually got word to British military stationed in the Gold Coast. The British were able to reorganize their troops and they sent in reinforcements and their main objective was to kill Yaa Asantewaa. However, they failed over and over again. It wasn't until they captured her daughter and threatened to kill her, that Yaa Asantewaa finally gave herself into the hands of the British. She was immediately exiled to Seychelles, the same Islands where the King was and she lived another 20 years and died there. The British never got their hands on the Golden Stool.

Queen Naa Asantewaa

Harriet Tubman

Chapter 6:   Queen Mother Harriet Tubman

Black women throughout history have been some of the greatest leaders that the world has ever known. When it came time for them to do a righteous act, they did not wait for the permission of white men to do so. During the days of American chattel slavery, many black women risked their lives trying to free themselves and their love ones from the bondage of white supremacy. None was more courageous and daring than Queen Mother, Harriet Tubman. She was one of the greatest and fiercest Black Queens that ever existed. Words cannot express the sheer power of this woman. Many of our white educators may have "grazed" over the history of Harriet Tubman, but none of them went into detail which deprives millions of black minds from the true story of this remarkable woman. Sure, they talked about her infamous paths to freedom, also known as the Underground Railroad, but they didn't tell us that she was so incredibly knowledgeable of secret routes that the federal government actually hired her as a guide and gave her military status. Why didn't our white teachers tell us this? We are talking about a black woman who was born into slavery who was so intelligent that she became a secret agent for the United States Union Army.

Born into bondage in 1820, Harriet Tubman had no knowledge of what freedom was. In fact, one could even question did she know what joy or happiness was in her youth. Her slave master was nothing short of pure evil. Although he did not physically punish her, he would hire her out to other white people who would do the punishing instead. They were turn out to be more abusive than her owner ever was. Many people believed that a slave could not do anything without first feeling the lash of the whip. Harriet was leased once to woman named, Ms. Susan, and she showed no mercy. People love to blame the brutal mistreatment of slaves on white men, but on the contrary. We must always remember, who are racist devils raising them? White women. One day, Harriet was taken from the field work. She was told by Ms. Susan that she would be a house servant from now on. There was a problem with that though. No one trained Harriet to properly do house chores and one can imagine how particular southern aristocrats were about their homes. Time and time again, Harriet would clean the house to the best of her abilities, but if she did one thing that was not to their standards, down came the whip on her tender flesh. Harriet was beaten over and over and over again for doing something wrong without ever being told how to do it right. That would harden any spirit and so it did Harriet's.

In today's society, we tend to think that "house slaves" somehow had it easy, because they worked in the house. This is a grave misunderstanding. No one had it easy, and in fact, in some situations it was the "house negroes" who were most traumatized. After Harriet served and cleaned up after white people from sunup to sundown, she then had to become a nurse at night and rock the white baby to sleep. God forbid if Harriet fell asleep while rocking the white baby to sleep, for is she did and the white baby cried out and awoke the mother, it was Harriet who would get punished and of course, it was under the sting of the whip. Now let's review. A little black girl was forced to do house chores all day for a white family and when it came time for everyone to sleep, she had to continue to stay up and rock the white baby throughout the night. If she did her chores wrong, she was whipped; if the white baby cried at night, she was whipped. What kind of hell is this? The life of a dog isn't as hard as that. What her foolish slave master failed to realize was, she was training Harriet from a young age to be able to endure sleepless and restless nights.

As time went on, Ms. Susie no longer cared to have Harriet around. Harriet's slave master hired her out to another buyer. It would be this new owner who would change her life forever. One day he dropped a weight scale on Harriet's head, breaking her skull to the bone. This injury would cause her to have visions and epilepsy for the rest of her life. She would fall into deep sleep at random times, and during these times, it was almost impossible to wake her. It was in the visions that she would have dreams of herself standing in open fields and across the open field were women stretching their hands out to her, pleading with her to come to freedom. Harriet was convinced. She had certain natural rights. She had the right to death and the right to liberty and it was her goal to have one of them by any means necessary. Serving white supremacy was no longer going to be an option of her. She would depend on these visions and her faith in God to lead her on the dangerous journey to liberation. She escaped.

The first time she escaped, she did so alone, only following the North Star and the "voice of God". She claimed that God spoke to her regularly and told her when to move and when not to move. When she arrived in the free states for the first time, she felt a wave of emotions and described how even the sun looked different from the eyes of freedom. She was not happy though. She was afraid. She had no welcoming party. She was a foreigner in a foreign land. She wanted her family there also and decided that she would not rest until all her family and love ones were set free. She knew if she stayed gone too long, with the slave trading business booming, there was always a chance that she would not see any of her relatives again. She knew that if she did not hurry and return, there was chance that's she would never see her loved ones again. She made up her mind and decided to go back and this time...she wasn't coming back alone.

19 trips. Harriet Tubman went into the pits of hell, that being the confederate south, 19 times and never lost a single person on the journey. Harriet Tubman single-handedly helped over 300 slaves escape to freedom. Name a white woman who went to an area 19 times and back to save her people knowing that she could have been enslaved and killed? The author will wait. So, the question remains, how did she do it?

Harriet Tubman may have been small in stature, but she was significantly stronger than your average man or woman. Even in her youth, when she was forced to carry branches and do other chores, her strength would amaze men that were onlooking. To deny black girls, this vast evolution of Harriet Tubman sends a clear message that the American education system is content with just knowing that Harriet was slave and she helped free other slaves. Yet, they fail to leave out that she was so physically strong, that she could do any job that a man could do. She was a warrior, a commander, a general, one who led by example and not just with words. She would leave maps and messages or send specific people to help other slaves escape. She could have did all of this from the comfort of her home in the North where she was allowed to be free, but no, she was right there with them, leading them from the trenches of hell, that being at the time, the southern confederate states of America. The question is how though? How did she become this infamous hero who lacked any sense of fear and weakness? She was molded that way. She was molded from the white family that she served and the lash of their whips. Their brutal torture and abuse on her, made her feel that risking her life for freedom was always a better option than accepting a day of slavery. She would work in Philadelphia, at hotels and shops. One day her fellow coworkers, asked her if she wanted to attend Uncle Tom's Cabin, a play about slaves and plantation life. Harriet declined and said she did not want to attend the performance of slaves because she had seen the real thing and there was nothing entertaining about it. She now longed for her family who were still enslaved in the south and she begin to set up a team of people to help her on her journey.

She traveled mostly by night and mainly by foot. Through rain, sleet, or snow, Harriet was determined to save lives. She went up mountains, through the forests, and even through muddy swamps. It was beyond an exhausting journey for someone who had never left a plantation. Many people tried to give up and even wanted to return to the plantations because they thought that volunteering to come back would be better than being captured by white people. Slaves who were almost free would be so tired that they would drop to the ground and cry out to her to leave them there and let them die. Her response to them would be "dead men tell no tales"..."go on or die". If a person would continue their plea for abandonment, Harriet Tubman would be so bold enough to raise a gun to their head and force them to move on. Now, how gangsta is that? It made sense too. If a slave was ever captured, they would be tortured to death until they gave up the secrets of Harriet Tubman and the Underground Railroad. If they wanted to die, they were going to do so right there at the hands of Harriet. Fortunately for them, continuing their journey to freedom was the most logical choice.

Out of the 19 trips, Tubman went all the way to Canada 11 times. She distrusted the American government so much that she wanted her people completely out of the country, especially after the passing of the fugitive slave law. The fugitive slave law stated that people in southern states and free states had to fully cooperate with the capturing of a runaway slave. If they were caught helping any slave, they would fined up to $1,000 or $29,000 today. The law was nothing short of evil and it was clearly directly right at her. A price was placed on her head for $40,000. Queen Harriet didn't flinch one damn bit, and she just decided to change her approach. From that point on, she would no longer travel during the day, but only at night and often times she would change her appearance to throw off onlookers. Overnight, Harriet Tubman without even trying became one of the greatest spies that the world had ever known.

Harriet was not just a warrior, but also a master scout, and a hustler. She knew she had to have money for her trips. When she first entered the north, she worked at hotels and shops at first. She would later enter hospitals and look for work, finding various ways to earn money. This was possible because it was during the time of the civil war, and there was non-stop work and injured patients. She would wash and help treat the bloody wounds of union soldiers from sunup to sundown and at night she would cook pies and breads and have them sold in military camps. Keep it mind, all of her money was mostly for her journey to free other slaves. When she was asked how did she keep going back to the south so fearlessly, she replied that she just trusted in God and if she died, she knew heaven was awaiting her for the righteous work that she was doing. She was a fierce woman to be reckon with.

Now news begins to spread about this remarkable black woman who had escaped from slavery and knew various routes unknown to any man. To black people, she was known as Moses, leading her people from bondage. The higher ups in the Union military eventually caught wind of her success and needed her help drastically.

Wars are won off 2 basic necessities: intelligence information and weapons. The union army had the weapons, but was severely lacking intelligence information. White southerners were beyond loyal to the confederacy and to compound that, some slaves were beyond loyal to their slave masters. Reason being, southern whites would manipulate slaves into thinking that northern "Yankees" were the worst creatures in the world. They would even say that northern whites had horns and tails to scare slaves from ever interacting with them. So the union had a problem. They needed someone who knew unknown routes into the south and they needed someone that slaves would trust when told that they were free. There was no one more qualified than Harriet Tubman.

She was hired by the military to assist in the dismantling of countless plantations and the freeing of thousands of slaves. She was aboard many gun boats that eliminated the final artillery in the south. When slaves saw the white men on the gun boats, they would flee into the forests out of fear that they were about to be harmed. They had no idea that the men on the boat were there to liberate them from their slave masters. It would only be the presence of Harriet Tubman that would ease the tension and help convince slaves that they were finally free men and women.

For 3 years of outstanding service of being a nurse, a master scout and a spy for the union army, she only received $200. At the end of the war, she went to court and demanded that she should be given the same pay as any veteran and made note that it was her expertise that help the union win the war without wasting time and money. She was denied time and time again. The only payment she was given was a widow's check earned by her former husband who served during the war. None of her outstanding work was ever properly compensated. She had been abused in the south, and now she was being used in the north. Used and abuse is the chorus that America loves to sing to black people. Nevertheless, Harriet had sought out to do what she had aimed to. She and her people were free and her lifelong story will forever be timeless. She was and will forever be a true American Queen.

Harriet Tubman

Maggie Walker

Chapter 7:   Pennies into dollars Maggie

In the hot bloody summer of 1865, Robert E. Lee, General of the Confederate Army surrendered to General Ulysses S. Grant and the Union Army. The day that black people had prayed for had finally arrived. Slavery in America, for the most part, had been abolished. For the first time in life, millions and millions of black Americans had a true taste of freedom. That freedom was not much freedom at all due to the fact that enslaved black people and their descendants were never given any reparations for the atrocities of chattel slavery. Due to the tyranny of white supremacist groups and job discrimination, black freedom and white freedom was not the same at all. Black men struggled to find work that didn't involve sharecropping. Black people would work from sunup to sundown picking cotton and may only take home $2 if that. As hard as it was for the black man to find work, it was 10x harder for the black woman. Nevertheless, as black women do, they persevered. Many black people knew that white America was not going to give them the solutions they needed to establish strong communities. No oppressor educates the oppress on how to defeat him. That would be counter-productive. Therefore, black men such as Booker T. Washington, founder of the Tuskegee Institute, made education the number 1 priority.

Young minds who were previously forbidden to read turned into sponges of knowledge. Black men became owners of oil companies and politicians in just a few years out of slavery. Black women were in the fight for knowledge and businesses too, and none more so than political activist, Maggie Lena Walker.

Maggie Walker was an American teacher, political activist, philanthropist, newspaper editor, and she was the first black woman to be president of an American bank. Her story is vital to young African-American boys and girls, but white educators with their white-washed curriculum, skip over her everyday and it's not by chance, it is intentional. They don't want us to know about our rags to riches stories, because it is their wish for us to stay in the rags. However, that could not be told to Maggie Walker.

Walker was born Maggie Elena Draper on July 15th, 1864. Her mother was a paid house maid for the American spy and abolitionist Elizabeth Van Lew. Her father was a white confederate soldier. Needless to say, he was not in her life at all. Maggie Walker was very light and had hazel eyes, but that did not grant her one favor. Her small shade of melanin was just enough for white people to condemn her to be naturally inferior. It didn't matter if our women was rich in melanin or hardly had any, if you had one drop of African blood, you were all given the titled "colored". Therefore, it is very foolish today to entertain such notions as "team dark skin" and "team light skin" when we are all being oppressed by the same white man. Oppressed or not, Maggie Walker was not going to let one damn thing stop her.

The beginning of her life was not easy by any means. As early as she could remember, she had to carry a wash basket on her head. Her mother had no education or trade skills, so she was forced to tend to the houses of white folks for little pay. One thing that kept Walker and her family positive was their strong faith in God. She grew up near a church in Richmond, Virginia and she attended service regularly. It was because of the church that Maggie Walker felt compelled to help her brothers and sisters in faith overcome the obstacles that was inflicting their community. From there, she was one of the first generations of black Americans to be allowed to attend public schools. Maggie Lena Walker took full advantage and excelled in school and realized that through education, Black Americans could save Black Americans. Through education, black people could teach liberation to black people, and that was the problem. Black people had not properly been taught how to manage their finances. Black people had never been taught before to have pride in their race and surely black people were never taught that they can someday ultimately defeat white supremacy. Maggie Walker understood all of this and it made her invincible.

Armed with knowledge, Maggie Walker wasted no time in calling out the hypocrisy of white supremacy. When it came time for her and her classmates to graduate school, they wanted to use a ballroom in the city that was paid for by the taxpayers. The city council denied them that right and told them that the ballroom was to only be used by white students. Maggie replied "Our parents pay taxes just the same as you white folks, and you've got no business spending big money out of those taxes to pay for the theater for white children unless you do the same for black children," (Branch and Rice). Her protest was the first African American school strike in history. From there, Maggie Walker became a master teacher and educated for 3 years at the former school that she attended. In 1886, she got married to Armstead Walker Jr., and had 2 sons. Unfortunately, in those days, women were not allowed to have a job and have a family. Social norms required that they make choice and obviously Maggie Walker chose her husband and children. Despite doing what was "the right thing" in those days, Maggie Walker was not going to let society box her in as just being a stay-at-home wife and mother. She had big dreams and real solutions and she was not going to be silenced by anyone. Since Walker was not permitted to teach, she decided to become influential in other areas. She joined a national black fraternal order known as the "The Independent Order of Saint Luke". These fraternal groups were used as institutions to help black communities pass valuable information and economic insurance. As time went on, the group begin to lose money and members. They were on the brink of closing permanently, but black women being black women, stepped up and took control of the situation. In 1901, Maggie Walker had climbed the ranks in the fraternity and she introduced a solution that would not only save the fraternal group from closing, but it would save black people as a whole. She called for a meeting and instructed the members that black people needed 3 things:

1   We need our own grocery stores.
2   We need our own newspapers.
3   And we we need our own banks.

She instructed that it all be ran under the title of "Independent Order of Saint Luke". It doesn't sound like much, but please understand the wisdom of this Queen. In 1901, only a few years out of slavery, Walker had already come to the understanding that that whoever controls information, controls the people and therefore, whoever controls the news, control the destiny of the people. In 1901, she came to the understand that if black people eat every day, why would they depend on white people for food? In 1901, she knew that it made no sense too, to give all of their money to the same banks who were aiding in oppressing them.

"First, we need a savings bank. Let us put our moneys together; let us use our moneys; let us put our money out at usury among ourselves, and reap the benefit ourselves. Let us have a bank that will take the nickels and turn them into dollars."
-Maggie L. Walker
Independent Order of St. Luke Annual Convention August 20, 1901

If Maggie Walker could understand all of that in 1901, why the hell can't black folks see that in 2019? Walker's speech was successful and soon after, she would purchase the St. Luke Hall in Jackson Ward of Richmond. Inside of the building were her private offices. Also inside, she had a treasury with a vault and the printing press of her newspaper, The St. Luke Herald. She became a Boss's Boss. Her influence could not be kept to Virginia solely. She now had the power to reach black Americans on a national scale.

The great thing that is admired about Maggie Walker was her raw eagerness to put black women to work and give them a fair shot at life. Black women made up the majority of her staff because she knew how hard it was for them to find work. Not only that, when black women did find work, they were usually assigned as wash maids and house servants only. Maggie Walker knew that black women and black men were not obligated to work for white people. She understood that the ultimate goal was to put all of our efforts into building our own communities and our own institutions, not the communities and intuitions of our oppressors. Because of this, Maggie Walker had the trust of black women. Instead of working the backbreaking, low paying jobs that white people had, under Maggie Walker, for the first time in life, black women had actual careers. Maggie Walker promoted black women from house maids and wash women to clerks, bookkeepers, typists, and stenographers. This made her a national hero to many. In 1903, Maggie Walker made more history. Just as she planned only 2 years prior, she opened the St. Luke's Penny Savings Bank. It was the first bank ever founded and ran by an African American woman. Her name had been written in history. The bank offered mortgages, checking and saving accounts, and investment loans to black entrepreneurs.

Black people were handling their business and acquiring so much wealth, that it intimidated the white people on the other side of town. These new prideful black people were seen in the eyes of their oppressors as "uppity negroes." Proof of that was the establishment the Jim Crow Laws. Under this racist and demonic legislation, black people were not permitted to step one foot inside of a white business. The few white businesses that did allow black to shop would not allow black people to try on the clothes before buying it. They feared that our beautiful brown skin would "ruin" the product. Maggie Walker questioned black folks that would dare spend their money where it is not wanted.

"Women of your race, your own flesh and blood, as polite and as capable as any other women on Broad Street, but they are Negro women,". She continued, "Some of you pass them by, preferring to feed the lion of prejudice rather than your own brethren. If we have the same shirts, cuffs and collars, underwear as the white stores, and we are not one cent higher, and in many instances cheaper, why spend your money with men who would not give your child employment except as a porter?" She added, "The only way we can kill the lion of race prejudice is to stop feeding him."

Oh, how relevant that is today. Walker's statement sheds light on the fact that black people begging black people to "buy black" is not anything new. It's only because white businesses are the most promoted and more modern, we rush to work for them and to buy from them. It's completely psychological and Maggie Walker understood that totally. No one should spend their time or their hard-earned money where it is not appreciated. Maggie Walker, being the courageous black Queen that she was, eventually bought a department store right on the same damn street as the racist white supremacist who denied their business to black people. She named it the St. Luke Emporium. She painted the mannequins black and for the first time allowed black people to try on clothes before wearing it. She was a force to be reckon with and white people had just seen the beginning.

In Richmond, streetcars were one of the major ways of transportation for black and white people. However, due to Jim Crow Laws, Black People had to give up their seats for white people at any given notice. This was in despite of the fact that they were paying the same amount of money. This is the insanity of white supremacy, to think less melanin makes you're more superior than someone with rich melanin. Since black people were not allowed to vote, Maggie Walker knew that the only chance of gaining respect and humanity was to change how they were spending their black money. She used her newspaper, the St.

Luke Herald, to reach the ears and minds of the black people in the community. She had one message for thousands of black people, "walk". She knew that although riding in a streetcar is comfortable and easy, self-pride was more important. So black people saved their streetcar money and begin to walk everywhere they needed to go. This is one for the first Africans-Americans boycott of a white business post slavery. After 2 years of boycotting, the streetcar company was forced into bankruptcy. Isn't that incredible? Black people were united for only 2 years and were able to force a white business into total bankruptcy. Today, it's hard for black folks to protest a week without being distracted by something that holds no concern to our community. Maggie Walker showed the power of the black dollar in 1904, so imagine how much more powerful the black dollar is now? She must be taught to our young, energetic minds so that we may all benefit from her marvelous works and teachings. More importantly, she must be taught to our black women, so that that they know that there is nothing that they cannot achieve if they put their mind and efforts into it. She was a leader, a fighter, and a hero to millions. We must never forget, before Black Lives Matter and Dr. Martin Luther King, Jr., there was Maggie Leana Walker leading boycotts. She was a master teacher and she used the power of the black dollar to put fear in the heart of white supremacy and pride into the heart of Black America.

Maggie Walker

Madam C.J. Walker

Chapter 8:   Unstoppable

Around the same time, Maggie Walker was leaving her footprint in American society, there was another Black Queen making some serious noise. Madam C.J. Walker was an American businesswoman, mother, wife, entrepreneur, political activist, black leader, and a philanthropist who was a slave as a child. How the hell could she not be considered "vital information" for young African Americans? The author will never know. Madam Walker was born in Delta, Louisiana, on December 23, 1867. Her birth name was Sarah Breedlove. The slave plantation that she was born on was the same slavery plantation that her parents had been confined to their entire life. As soon as she was old enough to walk, Madam Walker was appointed hard labor. She begins picking cotton in the scorching heat at the tender age of 4. Even though she was merely a child, she was appointed no favors in life. By the time she reached the age of 7, both of her parents had died. Everyone who was a slave was vulnerable, but to be a 7-year-old slave child with no parents, one cannot put into words what that must have felt like. When she reached her teens, she wanted to have a home of her own and she wanted to escape her cruel brother-in-law which insinuates that there may have been some sort of trauma or abuse that was taking place. At age 14, she got married and at age 17, she had her only daughter A'Lelia Walker.

When she reached the age of 20, more hardship would take place. Her husband of only a few years died, and now Madam Walker was once again left unprotected, except now, she had a baby. Her back was against the wall. Moving back in with her sister and brother-in-law was not an option because of the abuse that had taken place years prior. Her only option was to turn to her brothers, who were all barbers in St. Louis. In most black communities in those days just as it is now, it was the black barbers of the communities who had influence and connections to everyone on all levels.

With no education or corporate training, Madam Walker job options were limited. For 18 long years, Madam Walker worked as a wash woman. Some days she struggled just to make $2. Around the 1890's, Madam Walker begin to lose her hair. Every day, it became thinner and thinner. She felt ashamed and embarrassed by this and desperately wanted to find a solution. Madam Walker was incredibly saddened by her situation and she said for 3 nights in a row, she had a dream about a big African man telling her what she needed to do to cure her scalp disease. Madam C.J. Walker made the formula and followed the steps precisely and it worked! Her hair begins to grow back healthier and more beautiful than it ever was. People begin to notice and asked her what her secret was. She begins to sell her formula around her community and that's when her life would change forever. Her natural business sense would begin to take over from there. She would go door to door showing black women before and after pictures of her hair and usually that's all it would take to make a sale. This technique "before and after" pictures, was mastered by her and the product was so good, that it practically sold itself. Madam Walker was getting rich and she was getting rich fast. To help the reader understand, Madam C.J. Walker acquired so much money that she eventually bought a house that was in the same neighborhood as Billionaire John D. Rockefeller. I repeat, a black woman who was a former slave, managed somehow, to buy and live beside one of the richest men that has ever lived. That's quite the journey. In 1906, Madam Walker founded her company and in 1910 she built a factory in Indianapolis. When she moved there, she realize that through philanthropy she could begin to have more influence in areas where black women had little. At the time, there was a campaign to build a black YMCA in the city, but they were lacking funds. Madam Walker donated 1k dollars which what would be equivalent to 25k today. The media went into a frenzy. It was the largest donation that any black woman had ever made to the YMCA. Madam C.J. Walker now had national attention and that's exactly what she wanted. As her status and wealth grew, so did her confidence and Madam Walker wanted to use her new found power for good. She wanted to improve the lives of African-Americans and she wasted no time in doing so. In 1912, Booker T. Washington held his annual National Negro Business League Conference in Chicago. Madam C.J Walker attended. In the early 1900's, Booker T. Washington founded the Tuskegee Institute and was the most powerful black man in America. Madam C.J. Walker did disagree with him on a few issues but did agree with him that education among black Americans was a top priority. When she got to the conference, she had instructed Washington's secretary that she would like to speak and provide some insight on how people can be entrepreneurs and how black women can help make a difference in the fight for nation building. She was ignored. Soon later, a prestigious gentleman by the name of George Knox, owner of the Indianapolis Freeman Newspaper, stood up in the audience and asked that Madam C.J. Walker be allowed to speak. He was also ignored. As the conference was ending, Madam C.J. Walker saw that she was not going to be allowed to speak. She decided to take matters into her own hands. She stood up in her chair and looked at Booker T. Washington right in the face said... "Surely you're not going to shut the door in my face, I am a woman who came from the cotton fields of the South. From there I was promoted to the washtub. From there I was promoted to the cook kitchen and from there I promoted myself into the business of

manufacturing hair goods and preparations....... I have built my own factory on my own ground."
— *Madam C. J. Walker, 1912*

The next year, Booker T. Washington made her the main event.

By the year 1919, Madam Walker had over 20,000 black women employed by her. Known as Walker Agents, these black queens for the first time in their life could have total control of their own business endeavors. Madam Walker had schools and classes throughout the nation teaching and grooming black women on how to be successful salesmen and business women. She gave out diplomas for the graduates of her schools and loved to give out bonuses to her top employees that did extraordinary work. She had become the epitome of the "rags to riches" and her effort to improve the status of black women in America inevitably improved the lives of Black America as a whole. Because of Madam C.J. Walker, single mothers still had a chance of obtaining much wealth on their own with no assistance from a man. This independence was a breath of fresh air for many black women who were facing job discrimination. Who today is looking out solely for the needs of black women? We don't know many. However, we know Madam C.J. Walker did and in doing so she looked out for the black community. Her story must never cease from being told. Each generation of black Americans is owed the knowledge of her incredible achievements. To hide this should be criminal. For black women like Madam C.J. Walker, she did not wait for a hero, she became one. She did lean on hope, she became hope and her legacy will live on forever.

Madam C.J. Walker

Fannie Mae Lou Hamer

Chapter 9: Black Revolutionary Angela Davis

In the 50's and 60's, America had a big problem. Black people were being oppressed left and right and they were finally tired of it. Men like Malcom X were saying, "The Ballot or the Bullet." Him and millions of other black Americans had made up their mind, that if they were not going to have peace, there would be no peace for nobody. Black people started waking up and there was a conscious shift that swept the nation. Former criminals and alcoholics were changing their lives around and joining organizations that would improve their community. Men rose up to national fame such as Dr. Martin Luther King Jr., Malcolm X, Huey P Newton, and Bobby Seal. All of this is mostly understood by the general public. What is not understood is the huge contribution Black Women gave to help destroy Jim Crow and other oppressive policies. Claudette Colvin and Rosa Parks boldly refused to give up their seats in segregated Montgomery, Alabama. These two queens sacrificed their very freedom to object oppression. What about Fannie Lou Hamer? My God, how did our white educators leave her out? This Queen lived in the rural parts of Mississippi. Mind you, this state that had the most racial lynching in U.S history. One of the reasons why they would lynch a black person was if they tried to vote. Well, Fannie Lou Hamer came to the startling conclusion that there wasn't a white man or white woman on Earth who deserved more God given rights than she had. Needless to say, she was going to make sure she voted. In August of 1962, she dared to register to vote. When she came home, her landlord fired her on the spot and kicked her off her property. He was quoted in saying "Mississippi isn't ready for that." Remind you, it was 1962. A few days later on Sept 10, she was shot at 16 times! All because she wanted to vote! It didn't stop there; this Queen was beyond determined. In the following year, in 1963, Fannie Lou Hamer and group of activists wanted to attend the Southern Christian Leadership Conference. Along the way, they decided to rest a little bit at a local diner. The white waitress refused their service because they were black. However, the group did not flinch. A local policeman walked inside of the cafe and took out his knight stick to scare the group out of the restaurant. Not wanting to deal with violence on such a positive occasion, the group thought it would be best to leave. As they did, a few members of the group decided to write down the tag number of the policeman. As they were doing this, more policeman rode up and that's when everything changed. They begin arresting every member of the group including Hamer. While in jail, the women were beating and stripped naked. Some were beating so bad they couldn't see or talk. This treatment by the police was frequent. Fannie Lou Hamer was once abused by the police so bad that it took her over a month to recover from the wounds. Some of injuries never fully healed. She was a warrior for freedom.

This was the reality that many of our parents and grandparents had to deal with. There was silent war going on and white supremacy was and still is trying to kill our kings and our precious queens. Black Queens like Fannie Lou Hamer was taking charge. There was no Queen on the front line more than former Black Panther member and black revolutionary, Angela Davis.

What is something that many of these black Queens in this story share? They grew up knowing what tyranny is firsthand. No one had to teach them what oppression was and what brutality was; they were bred in it, they lived it. Similar to Harriet Tubman, and many other black women, Angela Davis was constantly being exposed to violence at a young age, forcing her to naturally think about the wellbeing her of people. Born January 26, 1944, Angela Davis and her family lived in in Birmingham, Alabama. During that time, Birmingham had a nickname, "Bombingham." Over a short period of time, nearly 80 bombs were set off in Angela Davis's middle-class neighborhood. Eighty! Once again, this is a specific detail that white American educators fail to leave out. White America always tries to stereotype Arabs when it comes to bombs, but in reality, it wasn't too long ago that they were the ones running around the country, blowing stuff up. To ignore this says something very specific. They don't mind letting you know some white people are evil, but they don't want you know "How" evil they can be. Once again, 80 bombs were set off in Angela's Davis community. That means people were scared while they were inside of their own home, while they were outside of their home, and even they were away from their home out of fear that it wouldn't be there when they came back. Can you imagine the psychological trauma that they must have endured? Davis even states herself, that as early as she can remember, bombs were constantly going off in her community. Her house would shake from the impact and once, a bomb was thrown into her neighbors house across the street from her. Newborn babies and children would be in the house. White supremacy did not care one bit. They bombed home after home to the point where Davis neighborhood was called "Dynamite Hill." This was all because a few black people were doing well for themselves and wanted a community of their own. Yet somehow, white people today will have the nerve to say, "we figured it out, why can't y'all." The response to that should be, "when we do figure it out, you all sabotage it."

The worst of these bombings would sadly occur on September 15, 1963. A bomb had been placed in the basement of 16th Street Baptist Church. White supremacy showed no mercy. The bomb went off, killing 4 young queens: Denise McNair, who was 11, and Addie Mae Collins, Carole Robertson and Cynthia Wesley who were 14. Their lives were cut short by a grown white man who had nothing better to do with his time. Angela Davis knew 2 of the girls personally and 1 lived next door to her. All of this violence and brutality propelled Angela Davis to be one of the great revolutionaries of all time.

The average person would probably be a little shell shocked from being exposed to so many bombings and killings at such a young age, but somehow Angela Davis still thrived in school. Like so many revolutionaries, education became an escape for her. She truly believed education was the way for the black Americans to unlock the psychological chains that had been placed on them by white supremacy. Davis did so well that she earned a scholarship to attend Brandeis University in Waltham, Massachusetts. She was one of the 3 Black People in her class. However, that was no pressure for her. After all, she was from "Bombington". That's pressure. Sitting inside of your home and not knowing if a bomb would go off at any many minute was real pressure. Eventually, she would meet a Frankfurt philosopher by the name of Herbert Marcuse. It was this man who instilled into Angela Davis, that it was possible to be a scholar, a professional and a revolutionary at the same time. She was so inspired by philosophy that she would later attend Frankfurt University. It was around this time, that the Black Panther Party begin to gain momentum and Angela Davis decided that she wanted to help their cause. She would move back to the states and soon earned a Master's Degree from the University of California and a Doctorate in Philosophy from Humboldt University in East Berlin. She was nothing short of a genius and that caused a problem for White America. Why did that cause a problem? Because they don't know what to do with people like that. What does America do with a black revolutionary who can't be classified as a "Thug" or "a gangsta"? What does America do with a black person who has been educated by white scholars and who has received master degrees from white universities and can still clearly see white supremacy for what it is? Nothing. There's nothing they can do, but watch them, and that's exactly what the U.S. government begin to do with Angela Davis.

Angela Davis had master degrees and doctorate degrees from white institutions and she was a professor at a predominantly white school. At the same time, she had an Afro touching both of her shoulders, speaking up for civil rights and she was raising her black fist every opportunity she got. To put it lightly, she was in your face about her blackness whether you liked it or not. She called it as many others did at the time, "a natural". She and Kathleen Cleaver, who we will talk about in the next chapter, decided to control the narrative of what beauty was for the black woman. Instead of promoting Eurocentric beliefs, they promoted self-love and self-acceptance.

President Ronald Reagan, who was then the governor of California, began to hear the news of a black professor at UCLA promoting black power and communism. Some black people thought communism was a better solution in a world of white supremacy because in capitalism, the power and the production is completely controlled by small group of people. The definition of communism is, "a theory or system of social organization in which all property is owned by the community and each person contributes and receives according to their ability and needs." Now to put it simple, there was wave of black people that was fed up with the norms of white America. They knew that this democracy did not live up to its definition. It was tyranny, plain and simple. They knew that capitalism was just a fancy word, for "white people keeping the money to themselves." So many turned to communism, and to many other social practices because they knew without a doubt that the system in

American was broken and only benefited one race. The governor of her state was Ronald Regan, and the president of the country was Richard Nixon and they both were watching Angela Davis closely. To give you an idea of what Nixon felt about black people at the time, his chief of staff, John Ehrlichman. is quoted in saying ..."The Nixon campaign in 1968 and the Nixon White House after that had two enemies: the antiwar left and black people. You understand what I'm saying? We knew we couldn't make it illegal to be either against the war or black, but by getting the public to associate the hippies with marijuana and blacks with heroin, and then criminalizing both heavily, we could disrupt those communities. We could arrest their leaders, raid their homes, break up their meetings, and vilify them night after night on the evening news. Did we know we were lying about the drugs? Of course, we did."

Angela Davis didn't give a damn. She continued to promote liberation despite being closely watched. On August 7, 1970, a 17-year-old black teen walked inside a courtroom in Marin County, California and took complete control. He gave the defendants guns and took the prosecutors and the judge as hostages. Later a shootout would take place, where the 17-year teen and the Judge were both shot.

Coincidently, days later, Angela Davis purchased the weapon that was used at a pawn shop. Somehow, the police department and even the Feds claimed that she must have had some connection to the courtroom incident. She was innocent, but she knew that any black person accused of shooting a white political figure was guaranteed the death penalty.

She decided to flee and stay with friends. Like Harriet Tubman, she only traveled at night. On August 18, J. Edgar Hoover placed this black college professor of UCLA on America's Top Ten Most Wanted List. Angela Davis's face was plastered all over the media. The FBI would eventually find her and good ole Nixon congratulated the Feds for the "capture of the dangerous terrorist Angela Davis." The public was enraged by the arrest and she gained national and even global outrage. Committees and countries all over the world worked together to free Angela Davis. She even had the support of mainstream entertainers which helped her cause greatly. After 18 months of incarceration, Davis was acquitted of all charges.

During her time in prison, she saw firsthand what the mass incarceration was becoming. When she was freed, she explained to the public, that they had to gain knowledge of the prison system and how it worked, and who it worked for. She explained that only 1% of prisoners in prison get a trial by jury. Many black people were in prison, guilty or innocent, simply because they could not pay the bail. Many prisoners were tricked by state defense attorneys who really did not want to take the case. White lawyers would convince black defendants to plead guilty and just serve a little time. However, in many instances, they would plead guilty and serve a lot of time. Angela Davis begin to expose these hypocrisies and gained more national fame for it. She predicted the systematic mass incarceration as it was just developing in the Nixon era and sure enough, she was right. Today, 1 in 3 black men will be systemically incarcerated, and that is not by chance or coincidence. It's Queens like Angela Davis who we must re-study to help destroy the mass incarceration that is destroying our communities today.

Angela Davis

Kathleen Cleaver

Chapter 10: Born to be a leader.
Kathleen Cleaver

There was another Queen in the Black Panther Party. Her name was Kathleen Cleaver. Strikingly beautiful, smart, and courageous, Kathleen Cleaver was a master at organizing and uniting black people. From a young age, she was bread to be a liberator. Her father and mother were both some of the first students at the Tuskegee Institute. Tuskegee is most famously known for being the first black university in America, which was founded by the world renowned, freedom activist Booker T. Washington. Because her parents worked at this prestigious university, they, of course, had a high level of consciousness and Kathleen Cleaver was young girl soaking it all up. Her father was hired to do some political work in India around the mid 1950's. He would take his whole family with him, including Kathleen. For the first time in her life, she witnessed a sight that she had never seen before. She saw people of dark skin in high positions in society. This was strange to see because she had been conditioned by the U.S. to only view black people in low positions. Until then, she had never seen beautiful dark skin people in high ranking positions of government. A little time after that, they would move to the Philippines. Once again, she would see many people of dark skin complexion in high ranking positions in society. So, what did that mean?

That meant that America was lying to the public about "skin color" being a reason why people are inferior. There was no relevant reason why skin color determined why a people couldn't vote. There was no relevant reason why skin color determined why a people couldn't govern themselves. This was just simply hate and white supremacy. While observing these new norms in foreign countries, her own father was highly evolved with trying to end segregation and imperialism globally. She paid attention to all of this. Her eyes were completely open. She knew that white supremacy was a destructive force, and she made it her life's work to destroy it.

Eventually, she would move back home in her high school years while her parents stayed abroad. She would attend the same school of legendary activist, Julian Bond, a highly known civil right leader who was also the one of the founders of the Student Nonviolent Coordinate Committee also known as "SNCC". SNCC was one of the most influential groups in the Freedom Riders and the March on Washington led by Dr. Martin Luther King Jr. Kathleen realized that if Julian Bond could lead the people, then she could do it too. During her last year of high school in 1963, all hell was breaking loose in the south. Kathleen saw an image of group of young black southern girls in the back of paddy wagon, singing. She was inspired right then and there. Young girls who were the same age as her were risking their lives for freedom and justice. She decided that she would do the same.

It was troubling times for black America in 1963. Birmingham was being bombed nonstop, MLK was in jail, the president of the United States John F. Kennedy was assassinated. Kathleen knew there needed to be drastic change. While attending college at Boneyard University, she was mentored by a man named George Ware, who was a chemist from Alabama. He also attended graduate school of Tuskegee University. He was highly engaged in politics and black liberation. He and another friend shared an apartment off campus and it was at that spot, that Kathleen would meet Stokely Carmichael, the father of the Black Power movement. Later should she would meet a gentleman who had a position in SNCC office in New York and he was in dire need of a secretary. He offered Kathleen Cleaver the job and she graciously accepted. She had wanted to be a member for years. Not too long after that, a longtime friend of Kathleen, Samuel Leamon Younge Jr. who was a military veteran was shot in the back and murdered by a gas station employee for simply trying to get black people to register to vote. He had joined the Navy right out of high school and was already a Veteran by the age of 21. He returned home and enrolled in Tuskegee and became highly invoked in the SNCC organization. When white supremacist saw that he was successfully getting black people to register to vote, they took action and assassinated him. George Ware was a mentor to Younge and was the one who encouraged him to join SNCC. He felt somewhat responsible and took the lost extremely hard. He was depressed and felt guilty. He decided to leave his job and he recommitted his life and time fully to SNCC. Ware decided to move back to Atlanta and he asked Kathleen to come work for him there. She accepted. The death of Samuel Leamon Younge Jr. was an important wake up call for black America. It made it clear that black people can put on a military uniform and go fight millions of strangers thousands of miles away, only to come back home and be murdered by the very people that you were sent to protect.

After moving to Atlanta, Kathleen had become very busy at SNCC. SNCC was becoming weaker due to financial problems. This was a direct consequence of Stokely Chamichel and other SNCC leaders taking a strong stance against the brutality of Israeli soldiers on Palestinian children. Many donors of SNCC were Jewish and even some of the members of the group was Jewish as well. After Stokely made his views public, the finances of SNCC dwindled down significantly. (This should be noted, many black liberation groups end up being funded by private

Jewish investors. This should be studied very closely as we know money is a tool used to control the interests of the masses.) It was due to the hard work, dedication, and sacrifices of Kathleen Cleaver that the group managed to keep on going despite having financial woes. She used her own personal money to help house key members of the group and constantly worked, taking notes and organizing events.

SNCC decided to have a conference in 1967 in Nashville, Tennessee called "Liberation Will Come from a Black Thing". Two problems arose.

1. At the time, white People were deathly afraid of Stokey Carmichael, despite the fact that he was only promoting liberation and freedom. They did not agree with the tone that he was using and it was no secret that he was the chairman of SNCC. So the school that was booked by SNCC backed out at the last minute leaving the group without a location.

2. The other problem was there was snow storm on the entire east coast. Airports were closing and key note speakers were canceling. They had no location and no speakers. Thankfully, a local priest volunteered his Church for the group to speak at. They still had no speakers though, except this one guy who was coming from

California, that man name was Eldridge Cleaver.

When Eldridge arrived in town, he went to the location that was hosting the event. Everyone there was extremely busy organizing the agendas for the audience. It was there that he would meet Kathleen Cleaver. He said that as soon as he laid eyes on her, it was love at first sight. Eldridge Cleaver was not your normal black leader though. He spoke unapologetically about his hatred for white supremacy and oppression. The conference was a success. A week after the conference ended, a riot broke out in town and Eldridge Cleaver was ordered by his parole officer to return home to San Francisco and to not leave. When Eldridge Cleaver arrived in San Francisco, he befriended a group of black people who were calling themselves the "Black Panthers". They were seeking total liberation from white supremacy. Soon after, Kathleen visited Eldridge and he introduced her to the Black Panthers and they all agreed on some strong issues. After the assassination of Dr. Martin Luther King Jr., it was evident that black people, even when being non-violent, could be killed at any given moment. Self-defense became the new priority and there was no other group promoting that more than the Black Panther Party out of Oakland, California. Similar to SNCC, the Black Panthers was totally against any oppression from white supremacy. However, they took more of a bolder stance on the matter. Unlike SNCC, they did not take on the motto of non-violence. They instead were in favor of self- defense. If you put your hands on a Black Panther or someone in their community, there were not going to march and sing gospel songs around you, they were going to meet you with equal force. White supremacy for the first time had to deal with armed black people who wanted their equality now, not later. Where a lot of groups such as SNCC focused on electoral and political matters, the Black Panthers were solely focus on organizing urban communities from within. They provided free breakfast programs for children and free groceries for impoverished families. Along with that, they patrolled black communities daily and would even follow policemen around to make sure that they were not physically abusing anyone. When Kathleen and Eldridge Cleaver joined the party, they had so much appeal to them that it became "cool" to be associated with the Black Panther Party. Black Panther demonstrations begin to take place all over the country. They were organized, armed and fearless and that scared the hell out of the majority of white America.

Now at this same time, America was at war. The U.S. declared that every American citizen who was a communist was a threat to the nation. Well check this out, at the same time that was being promoted, the Black Panthers were traveling to foreign countries and meeting with up with some of the top communists in the world. They knew America had no right to judge any other nation with the innocent blood that's on its hands. Kathleen and Eldridge Cleaver begin to set up international Black Panther parties in communists' countries. This enraged the federal government and caught the eye of FBI director J. Edgar Hoover. Hoover, known to be racist, once said, "Beware of the Black messiah" is his Coin Tel Pro documents. He was afraid of anyone that could possibly unite black revolutionaries on a global scale. That's exactly what the Black Panthers were doing and Kathleen Cleaver was doing all this while looking like a world super model. She had an Afro that would command the attention in any room. When asked about her hair, she explained how the black woman does not need to conform to European standards. She promoted that black women were perfect in their natural state and were the epitome of beauty.

So, the Panthers were busy organizing and the U.S. government was busy watching them. They had seen enough. They tried to dismantle the Black Panthers from the very top. Huey P. Newton was the leader of the Black Panthers. They made an assassination attempt on his life, but he was only wounded and lived. They were not done yet though. During that incident, a white officer had been shot and they wanted to give Huey P. Newton the death penalty for it. There was panic amongst the Panthers and chaos was on the brink of breaking out, but one Queen stepped up and took control. Being involved in SNCC, Kathleen Cleaver knew the power of demonstration. She knew that a successful demonstration had the power to gain national attention. She helped organized groups and held rallies in support of Huey P. Newton. White America could not believe what they were seeing. For the first time, they were witnessing, young, armed, articulate, and incredibly smart black youth who were demanding that their leader be set free. The demonstration was a success. It gained national attention and it was clear they Huey P. Newton was acting in self-defense. Had it not been for the leadership and quick thinking of Kathleen Cleaver, Huey P. Newton, the co-founder and leader of the Black Panther Party, would have been found guilty. Cleaver saved his life.

Kathleen Cleaver

Shirley Chisholm

Chapter 11: Before Obama, there was Shirley Chisholm

Time and time again, Black American women have defied the odds. Their power is unique and unmatched. There is no limit to what a black woman can do once she put her mind to it. That was evident in 1972, when a petite black woman, by the name of Shirley Chisholm ran for president of the United States. A few black men had ran for president of the U.S. in the past, but white America did not see that as a real threat, as they knew that majority of white America would never vote for a black man in those days. Frederick Douglass ran President in 1872. Eldridge Cleaver, as discussed previously, ran for president. Comedian, Dick Gregory ran as well and he even had money with his face printed on it and it was identical to U.S. currency. He was even threatened to be indicted on federal charges because of the public stunt. When asked about the money, Dick responded, "the bills couldn't be considered U.S currency because everyone knows a black man will never be on the U.S. Bill." It was all laughs and jokes. However, when Shirley Chisholm entered the scene, the jokes stop. Yes, there were a handful of black people who dared to run for president in the past, but not a single one had the resume' that Shirley Chisholm had. Shirley Chisholm was not a affiliated with any revolutionary groups that could be considered dangerous. Shirley

Chisholm was not a comedian trying to prove a point. No, on the contrary, Shirley Chisholm was the first black woman elected to the house of Congress. She represented New York's Congressional District since 1969. Being a democrat, she was a representative of a major political party. Shirley Chisholm's presidency was to be taken seriously, especially since she had already beaten the odds so many times before.

Chisholm was born on November 30, 1924, in Brooklyn, New York. Her mother was a seamstress and her father was a laborer. Finances become difficult after a while and Shirley was sent to Barbados to live with her grandmother. It was under the care of her grandmother that she would learn self-worth and self-love. In Barbados, the schools were much smaller, but this made Shirley's thirst for knowledge only stronger. After a few years, she moved back to New York. When she got back to New York, she was a lot smarter than most of her peers because the British education in Barbados was much stricter that the U.S. American education system. She would later enter Brooklyn College and excel there. There was only a small amount of black people in the entire school. Once, a Colombian professor saw her give a debate and was in awe of her passion and intellect. He urged her to enter into the world of politics. She obliged.

Now Shirley had two problems; politicians were generally white, and they were normally men. To be black and to be politician was revolutionary, but to be a black woman in politics was unheard of. Nevertheless, Shirley Chisholm pursued on.

Black women had been famous and powerful in the past before the 70's, but most were always held back due to racist legislation and bias politics. However, after the voting rights bill passed on 1964, it become possible that a black person could be anything they wanted to be without a federal government using race to hold them, back. No one understood this more than Shirley Chisholm. After winning her seat in Congress, she became a household name. She was a national hero to black women. She made it clear that she did not just support the progress of black America, but she supported the progression of all America. She did not just want to represent one race, but she wanted to represent all races. She wanted America to be what it was, a diverse nation of with many cultures and many nationalities. She was beloved by many for her unbiased views. In 1972, she announced her presidency for President of the United States:

"I am not the candidate of black America, although I am black and proud, I am not the candidate of the women's movement of this country, although I am a woman, and I am equally proud of that.....I am the candidate of the people of America."

She ran on the campaign of "Unbossed and Unbought", reinforcing to the nation that she was going to be a leader of all people. Her presidency gained momentum and it was clear that it was not a gimmick or a stunt. Millions of Americans truly believed that she could win. Unfortunately, she did not win, but what she showed to millions of black girls was still incredibly powerful. She proved that with hard work and dedication, anything for a black woman is possible.

The sad fact of the matter is, the author cannot remember one detail or fact about Shirley Chisholm that was taught in grade school or university. What kind of education is this? To be denied the knowledge of knowing that a black woman ran for president of the United States just a few years after gaining the right to vote. They told us bits and pieces of Harriet Tubman, but not a word about Shirley Chisholm. One came from slavery, and the other was running for president of America. They are equally important, so to teach the story of Harriet Tubman and deny the story of Shirley Chisholm sends a clear message. White America does not mind us knowing that we come slavery. However, they don't want us imagining ourselves as leaders of this country.

Shirley Chisholm

Coretta Scott King

Chapter 12: Summary

Throughout the history of man, the black woman has always been strong when her nation needed her the most. From the Nubian Queens of Africa to our ancestors in the Transatlantic Slave Trade, down to Representative Shirley Chisholm, black Queens have defied the odds repeatedly. There is no stopping a black Queen who puts her mind to something. The proof of that is in her own history. A history that is meticulously hidden from minds of young black queens by white supremacy. They know if you knew of the history of Queen Zewditu of Ethiopia, you might see yourself as a Royal Queen also. They understand that if you know the history of the great black Queens who lead nations to fight white supremacy, such as Queen Nzinga of Angola, Queen Yaa Asantewaa of Ghana, and Queen Amanirenas of Nubia, you might find the courage within yourself to do the same. Yes, that's what they fear. They never want to face a great Queen warrior like Queen Nzinga and Queen Yaa Asantewaa ever again, so they dare not teach about them. They know that the black woman has the ability to unleash the power of God on their heads if she is provoked to do so. That's why white supremacy would rather have her at the war with her fellow black man than with them any day of the week.

The principles and morals of black women from their history is based on righteousness. You take Maggie Walker and Madam C.J. Walker for example. These 2 Black Queens knew that black people had to control their own finances if they were ever to be truly free. It was a problem to be working for white people, spending money on white people and then having those same people oppress you every day. Both of these women were children of slaves, but they had enough willpower and tenacity to become 2 of the wealthiest black women of their time, mainly because they focused on the needs of their own people. Surely, if a black woman in the early 19th century can control almost 100% of the black hair owned products, a black woman today with all the resources we have, can do the same. How is it that we have gone from Madam C.J. Walker being the number 1 seller of black hair products to people of Asian descent being the number 1 seller of black hair products? You think that just happens? Of course not. It was systematic. Once we get control and produce the products that we use the most, then we must study Maggie Walkers history and put our black money in black banks. Once black queens learn more of about their history of governing nations and creating economies, they will naturally want do the same today, for it is within them do so.

Governing is natural for black queens, creating economies is natural for black queens, and providing security is also natural for black queens.

Reason being, since the dawn of time, black queens "don't take crap." Where there is unrighteousness, history has shown repeatedly, that a Black Queen will always be there to call it out. Take Queen Yaa Asantewaa of Ghana. When the European governor asked to sit and take the Golden Stool, the very "spirit" of their Kingdom, Queen Yaa Asantewaa lost it. She was ready to stand toe to toe with white supremacy and to go to war, no questions asked. We see this same spirit rise up in Angela Davis and Kathleen Cleaver in the 1960s. The black woman has a natural extinct to protect her community by all means necessary which is nothing short of righteous. This is obvious in the case of Queen Mother Harriet Tubman who put her life on the line numerous times for the sake of her people.

The black woman is 2nd to no one. If it was not for her, no person would be on this earth. She is the mother to all men and she should be adored as such. Praises are owed to the black woman for all that she is and all that she has had to endure. Through it all, she has been graceful. She is to be appreciated and most importantly, she is to be protected. This is an ode to the Black Queen; you are truly God's greatest creation.

Black queens you should know

Sojourner Truth (1797-1883)

abolitionist and women's rights activist, known for her famous writing, "Ain't I a Woman?"

Dr. Mary McLeod Bethune (1875-1955)

American educator, stateswoman, philanthropist, humanitarian, and civil rights activist best known for starting a private school, Bethune-Cookman, for African-American students in Daytona Beach, Florida

Gwendolyn Brooks (1917-2000)

poet, author, and teacher. Through literature she was able to express some of the struggles in the black community.

Bessie Coleman (1892-1926)

First woman of African-American descent to hold a pilot license.

Lena Horne (1917-2010)

American singer, dancer, actress, and civil rights activist. Fought vigorously against racism in the entertainment industry.

Billie Holiday (1915-1959)

Jazz singer who recorded the timeless hit, "Strange Fruit". White folks at the time called the song...a declaration of war.

Diane Nash (1938-present)

American civil rights activist, and a leader and strategist of the
student body section the Civil Rights Movement.

Hattie McDaniel (1893-1952)

Stage actress, professional singer-songwriter. Won the Academy Award for Best Supporting Actress, the first Academy Award won by a black actress.

Ella Baker (1903-1986)

African-American civil rights and human rights activist. Worked right beside Dr. Martin Luther King Jr. and was one of the most important women in the Civil Rights Movement.

Katherine Johnson (1918-present)

Nicknamed the Human Computer, this mathematician was the brain of calculating trips for NASA.

Mahalia Jackson (1911-1972)

Legendary gospel vocalist who became the soundtrack of the Civil Rights Movement. Whenever Dr. Martin Luther King Jr. called her to attend an event, she was always there, even if it meant that she had to travel to the deep parts of the racist south.

Dr. Patricia Bath (1942-present)

Ophthalmologist, inventor, humanitarian, and academic. She is the pioneer of laser cataract surgery.

Assata Shakur (July 16, 1947-)

- former member of the Black Panther Party and the Black Liberation Army. She led the Harlem division.

Made in the USA
Monee, IL
09 August 2023

40685124R00080